D1468470

love spells

love spells

Teresa Moorey

RYLAND
PETERS
& SMALL

LONDON NEW YORK

Senior Designer Sally Powell

Editor Miriam Hyslop

Picture Research Emily Westlake

Production Patricia Harrington

Art Director Gabriella Le Grazie

Publishing Director Alison Starling

Editorial Consultant Christina Rodenbeck

First published in the
United States in 2003
by Ryland Peters & Small, Inc.
519 Broadway, 5th Floor
New York NY 10012

www.rylandpeters.com

10 9 8 7 6 5 4 3 2 1

Text, design, and photographs
© Ryland Peters & Small, Inc. 2003

ISBN 1 84172 516 1

Printed and bound in China

contents

6   how to use this book

8   love tools

14   once upon a time

22   calling romeo

34   mirror, mirror

42   luscious lust

50   wedding bells

58   moving on

64   credits

How to use this book

Feel that it needs more than a new hairdo to make that love thing happen? You've come to the right place! On the following pages, you will find spells for lust, love, and wedding bells, designed to get you your heart's desire.

Start with "Love Tools" to suss it all out and get stocked up. Read the advice in each of the sections, so you understand what's important—and then it's all systems go on the astral plane, to draw that cutie close.

Just remember, never try to influence another specific person, and harm none—especially yourself.

And have fun!

love tools

A love witch needs her box of tricks—and the ingredients of love spells are delightful: strawberries, roses, and jasmine oil; good wishes, magic, and rhyme…

your love goddesses

We all need a little help at times, and there's plenty on hand from the divine realms when you're in search of romance. The Great Mother smiles on love and pleasure. Here are a few of her right-hand girls to give you guidance.

Greek APHRODITE is the most loved-up goddess. She is a flagrantly sensual temptress, right behind you when you're on the prowl and set to seduce.

VENUS is the Roman equivalent of Aphrodite. Herbs and stones used in love-spells are usually ruled by the planet named after her. She is the radiant queen of every loving encounter.

ISIS was the life-giving goddess of ancient Egypt. Call on her for power, fulfillment, and fertility.

YEMAYA is the African goddess of the sea and cycles. Beautiful and mighty, she is your ally when you need to change.

FREYA is the Norse goddess of sexual power and the joy of intimacy.

HERA is the Greek goddess of marriage and committed relationships.

Take your pick!

attracting love energy

surround yourself with jasmine, candles,

incense and essential oils
rose, jasmine, ylang ylang, patchouli,
vanilla, thyme, basil, cardamom,
cinnamon, coriander, lavender, copal

flowers
rose, geranium, violet, orchid,
hyacinth, gardenia

fruits
apple, strawberry, pomegranate,
tomato (love apple)

candles
rose, soft blue, red, pink, white

stones
rose quartz, lapis lazuli, emerald,
amethyst, turquoise, amber,
moonstone, topaz

images and objects
hearts, doves, swans, Cupid,
your darling, loving couples, the
Chinese love knot, wedding
photographs, love poetry

roses, orchids, strawberries, hearts ...

Love magic can be all around you—all the time.
Turn your bedroom—or your whole home—into
a love-den by surrounding yourself with those
special things that are sure to please the gods
and goddesses of love. Try adding red or pink
to your decor to encourage good love vibrations.

once upon
a time

Every love story begins in the same way. First boy has to meet girl, then the age-old dance of flowers and romance can begin…

Clubbing or classes, outings or the office?
Where's the best place to look for that lover?

a bag of precious stones

to help you find a lover

Name a stone for each possible venue. Go with what you feel, but some suggestions are: agate for evening class, onyx for the office, lapis lazuli for a party, carnelian for clubbing, moonstone for family events, garnet for sport, jade for dining out, and aquamarine for anything kooky. Put all the stones in the bag.

When you want to look for your lover, burn your pink candle and relax with some music and your favorite drink. Mentally ask your question and shake the bag. Without looking, put your hand into the bag. The stone you draw out tells you where to look for love. It may be appropriate to draw several—however, the first drawn should take priority when you have a choice. Re-draw again after a few months if you need to. Happy hunting!

Who is your romantic future? Here's how to open your inner eye.

the likely lover

to see your future partner

you will need:
a candle
a dark bowl filled with water
jasmine essential oil or incense
a pen and a piece of paper
some rose tea

Make sure the room is dark. Light the candle so that its flame reflects on the water. Burn the oil or incense of jasmine.

Ask to be shown your lover and let yourself enter a dreamy state. Gaze deep into the water. Images and shapes will form, either in your mind or seemingly in the water itself.

If you are very lucky, or skilled, you may see a face. But you are more likely to see symbols—for instance, ships could mean a sailor or a seaside meeting. Write down everything you see and check it out later.

A few drops of jasmine oil on your pillow or rose tea drunk before bed will make you dream of your love.

your love scroll

wish for your heart's desire... you can't get

This is a good spell to do once a year, as your preferences may change. If possible choose the Beltane festival, in early May, for this marks the beginning of the "loving season."

what you want until you know what it is!

you will need:
a pink candle

several sheets
of pink paper

a pen that looks
attractive and writes
smoothly

some lavender oil

some deep pink
satin ribbon

Light the candle and focus on the kind of lover you desire.

If you have a previously written list, burn it in the candle flame before you start.

Now write a list of all the qualities you seek in a beloved. Make a rough list first if you like. Think about what would make you comfortable and enhance your self-esteem, rather than romantic fantasy. For instance "big, blue eyes" will lose their charm if the person behind them is selfish. Someone who supports and understands you may be better than excitement.

Complete your list carefully—you may want to sleep on it and finish it the following evening. When you are sure, dab some lavender oil at the corners of the paper, roll it up, and secure with the satin ribbon. Keep the scroll somewhere safe, and when doing any love-magic in the future, place it near you.

calling romeo

Hold a seashell to your ear and ask a question about your love. Listen carefully for the whispers in the shell—do they give you your answer?

love is all around

attracting love vibes

Love is all around you—it is, in fact, the Goddess, who is close to us in every sunbeam, every tree, every flower and raindrop.

Witches honor nature. Every spell is an act of worship, using the beautiful things we have nearby to "spell out" our deepest wishes.

To attract love you need to be open to it first. Let the spells you do make you conscious of the fabulous gifts we have been given, just by being alive.

All the world loves a lover—be in love with life and you'll be spoiled for choice!

Beautiful rose quartz opens the heart of the person wearing it and draws to them all sorts of loving vibes. You can wear it as jewelry or carry it in your purse or pocket.

making a love talisman

Surround yourself with images of love. Light the candle and burn the incense.

Because you are "charging-up" a charm, you need a psychic haven, so imagine all negativity leaving you and your surroundings as gray clouds. Imagine a protective "egg" of pink light around you. Press your rose quartz between your palms and repeat your intention at least three times. Dance around, if you wish.

When you have finished, ground yourself by eating and drinking something you like. Imagine your "egg" dissolving.

Wear your charm whenever you need to attract that loving vibe.

you will need:

images of love, for example, kissing couples, doves, hearts, flowers, rings, a love scroll (see p 20)

an image of Venus to keep you company

a deep pink or rose candle

jasmine or rose incense

a piece of rose quartz that feels right for you—a heart-shaped one would be ideal

something to eat

Even though you are sure you want love, your heart might be sealed against it. Unlocking your heart isn't a physical matter, but instead needs you to open your heart chakra.

chakra power

to awaken love energy

you will need:
thyme and rose incense

wear emeralds if you have them, or try an emerald green scarf placed across your chest

green candles

Your chakras are the spiritual energy-centers in your body. There are believed to be seven altogether, and they are each associated with a color of the rainbow. The heart chakra is green, and it is situated in the chest. Opening your chakra may take some practice.

In a quiet place, light the incense and make yourself comfortable. Imagine you are drifting over lush green fields. The world is radiant, peaceful, and beautiful. Feel the love of nature fill you, making you joyful. Imagine the color green gathering in your chest and flooding your being. Feel trustful in the process of life.

Try this exercise sitting with your back against a tree. Feel the warmth of the tree seeping into your body.

Light a green candle every evening until you feel your heart is peacefully opening.

Remember it is important not to do spells to directly influence someone else—so you're walking a fine line here! It's okay to make yourself noticeable and sexy, but if you're targeting a specific love, you could be asking for trouble. You have been warned!

lust magnet
to get attention

you will need:
some natural vanilla oil

a red candle

a magnet

a piece of clothing or jewelry that emphasizes a physical asset, for instance, a choker, a see-through lace blouse, or stockings

Rub the vanilla oil into the candle and the magnet, and put just a tiny drop on your chosen garment. Light the candle and imagine yourself crackling with sex appeal. Wrap the garment or jewelry around the magnet and pass it clockwise around the candle three times saying:

"Lust magnet, lust magnet, lust magnet."

Wear your charmed piece—strut your stuff!

Remember, it's best to work on yourself instead of a target lover—so YOU'LL be enchanting! Who knows what else you'll catch in your net?

love incense

to enchant a lover

Mix the dried rose petals, dried thyme, and jasmine oil together, imagining how you will feel when you know you are utterly enchanting. Think about adoring gazes, compliments, caresses.

Light six rose-colored candles and play smoochy music. Place the image of Aphrodite beside one of the candles. Light some charcoal in a censer and sprinkle on enough incense to give off curls of vapor.

Waft the incense around you so the coils of smoke envelop you. They are infusing you with the power to enchant. If you've got very good reason—don't kid yourself—to think he's already keen on you, place something showing his initial or astrological sign or something belonging to him in front of you and waft the censer in a figure-of-eight that encircles his symbol and then you, in one motion.

you will need:

some dried rose petals

some dried thyme

jasmine oil

six rose-colored candles

dreamy sexy music

a picture or statue of Aphrodite

some charcoal and a censer (you can get these from New Age shops)

Mirror Mirror

Who's the fairest of them all?
Become beautiful in your own eyes and
you will be irresistible to your darling.

It's time to make the most of your natural talents. You've got the right to be the best "you" possible—luscious, lovely, cool, and sexy.

being irresistible

luscious, lovely, cool, and sexy...

But always remember that witches seek "power to," not "power over." However tempting it may be to try to bag that lover, please don't! Why? There are several reasons. First, it isn't ethical to tamper with the life path of another. Second, you can never be sure who's going to be right for you. That tall, dark Romeo could be the mad axman—or just boring!

So keep your spells general, for the right person for you, not a specific person. Leave the rest to the experts —the Gods of love and lust!

After this bath, you'll be too lush to leave alone.
Forget "beauty is in the eye of the beholder"—
beauty is in the thigh of the beheld!

beauty bath

bring out your inner Venus

you will need:
six crimson candles

vanilla essence

dried or fresh rose petals

scented body lotion

Light the candles in your bathroom and run a warm bath, imagining as many sexy scenarios as you can and sending them out into the ether with the steam. Add several drops of vanilla essence to the water and scatter on the rose petals. Lower yourself into the welcoming bath.

Watch the fire of the candle flames dancing on the water. This fire is now within you—you're red hot! Feel beauty and desirability saturating you from the magical water. Caress yourself gently, affirming you are beautiful, imagining the touch of a lover replacing your own hands. List all your good points. Let your imagination play with as many positive and sexy images as you like and feel these seeping into you.

When you are ready, dry yourself— preferably with a luxurious crimson towel. Rub in your lotion, so sealing the magical effects of the bath, within you. Put on the ritz—and get ready to fight 'em off!

We are all surrounded by swirls of colored light, which describe our personality and mood. This is called an aura, and it may extend as much as six feet from the body. Although most of us can't see auras, we all sense them. This is what makes some people more inviting than others.

an aura of love

to draw love in

you will need:
a glass of spring water
(from a bottle is fine)

natural red food coloring (beet juice would be good)

an image of a goddess

a wine-red cloth

To charge up your aura, leave a glass of spring water in the light of the full moon. Place a few drops of natural red food coloring in the water, so it turns pink.

Place your effigy of Venus, Aphrodite, or Isis before you on a wine-red cloth. Say:

"Great goddess, surround me with love."

Drink the water, imagining it filling your body with love-energy that sparkles outward, making your aura a warm, come-and-get-me pink. Prefer another color? If soft blues and greens mean love to you, coordinate your spell accordingly. The goddess isn't fussy!

luscious lust

Use this clutch of delicious spells to lead your lover up the garden path—a scented garden of sensual delight, that is.

Brew your potion on a Friday
when the moon is waxing.

love potion

to kindle lust

you will need:
a cup each of fresh strawberry juice,
pear juice, and cherry juice (apple juice
may be used as a substitute)

a copper pot (if possible)

an apple

six cardamom seeds

a vanilla pod

raw cane sugar

Place all the juice in the copper pot
with an apple, cut in half crosswise to
show the five-point star at the center.
Simmer the juices very gently for five
minutes with six cardamom seeds and
a vanilla pod. If possible, keep the apple
halves facing up.

Sweeten to taste with raw cane
sugar and leave out in the moonlight
for half an hour.

You can add spring water to your
potion, or mix it with wine before drinking.

That special date's coming up and you could do with a boost from the occult realms!

hot date

bringing Mars and Venus together

you will need:
two small effigies, one for you and one for your lover—chess pieces will do

a goddess figure

daisies or sprigs of mint

a red candle

a piece of jewelry containing carnelians

Place the effigies in front of your goddess figure—Isis, Aphrodite, Venus, or Freya will all bless you. Entwine all three figures with daisies or sprigs of mint, paying special attention to strong links between the effigies.

On the candle, carve the Venus symbol and the Mars symbol entwined. Place the jewelry around the base of the candle—if it is a ring, place it touching the candle.

Light the candle and let it burn down—you can do this on successive evenings. But if you only have a little time before you go out, burn it for as long as you can.

Wear your carnelian—and get set to smolder!

all night long

make your bed a hot bed

A night of passion should be perfect in every detail. Call on the goddess of love for help.

you will need:

pink or red sheets

a sprig of southernwood, mint, or rosemary

an image of a goddess

two deep red candles

rose, jasmine, or cinnamon oil or incense

some roses

spring water

red wine

a rose joss-stick

Make your bed with sheets of pink or red. Place a sprig of southernwood beneath the bed. A sprig of mint or rosemary will also keep things spicy.

Lighting should be very soft. Flank your goddess-image with two deep red candles and face her toward the bed. Burn some oil of rose, jasmine, or cinnamon—or a blend of these you have tested for unique scent.

Place large vases full of fragrant roses around the room and, if possible, allow the light of the moon to fall upon the bed.

Two glasses should be put on the bedside table, with spring water, wine, and, of course, some love potion, just in case you need it!

Before the night-to-remember, sit on the bed, mentally blowing away all negativity. Now cast a love-circle around the bed by circling it with a rose joss-stick. Sprinkle the bed with a very little rose oil and lie on it for a while, thinking very sexy thoughts! Now trace Venus and Mars shapes on the sheets and affirm that you are drawing everything sexy the Cosmos has to offer into this space.

Sleep well the night before—you'll need your rest!

wedding bells

All the best stories end with these words:
"...and they lived happily ever after..."
Make it so with these special spells.

A mandala is a circular design symbolizing wholeness. If you make a mandala of your love, your subconscious mind will be encouraged to foster your relationship. So much the better if your lover makes it with you.

making a mandala

you will need:

fidelity—amethyst and dried clover

fun—amber and dried St. John's Wort

fertility—holey stone and acorn

shared goals—lapis lazuli and lavender

money—coins and oak leaves

home—moonstone and a picture of your house

health—topaz and juniper

sex—carnelian and some cinnamon sticks

Improvise to your heart's content.

Your mandala can be a drawing, a collage, an arrangement of semiprecious stones—even a flowerbed! Divide your circle into an even number of sections—eight is a good number. Here is a suggestion.

Pin hawthorn twigs on a board, forming a circle. Divide into eight sections with twigs. Embellish the sections (see left) for fidelity, fun, fertility, shared goals, money, home, health, and sex.

On an anniversary or festival or at full moon, burn four candles around your mandala and celebrate.

To keep your relationship fresh and magical, renew your vows each year. Choose a time when the moon is waxing. Go to your favorite grove or stone circle, if you like. Or have a party and invite your friends.

you will both need:
a list of all the things you love about your partner

a lavender ribbon

amethyst jewelry

seeds (poppy seeds are a good choice)

renewing your vows

anniversary spell

First name the things you aren't quite happy with in the relationship, and ask your lover if these can change. Be prepared to change in return. Take the list of things you especially love and appreciate about your partner, including anything special they have done over the past year. Tie it into a scroll with lavender ribbon and swap. Exchange amethysts, or amethyst jewelry—this could be the same two pieces passed back and forth.

Plant the seeds together, in a circle or heart shape. Affirm that you will tend the seeds jointly.

Have a celebration together!

Sometimes you need some brand-new magic to help you get rid of a lousy lover. Don't hesitate to eliminate Mr. or Ms. Wrong.

turnip off!

getting rid of unwanted attentions

Being pestered by Mr./Ms. Wrong draws
your energies away from their real
purpose—finding Mr./Ms. Right!
Which bit of "No" doesn't he or she
understand? This spell will sort it out.
Do this spell when the moon is waning.

you will need:
a black candle

patchouli oil or incense

a turnip or other root vegetable

a sharp knife

black thread

Remember, this spell is to stop someone from making your life unhappy—nothing more.

Light the candle and the incense. Cut a large piece of the turnip and write on it with a sharp knife or compass point:

"......, leave me alone, signed ....."

Imagine the person turning away from you, attending to something else.

Bind the black thread around the piece of turnip at least four times, and knot it securely.

Bury the turnip when the moon is waning.

healing a broken heart

a spell to the Lady Moon

If your heart has been broken, then you are
ill just as surely as if you have a physical
malady—so treat yourself gently.

Do this spell when the moon is waxing to full. Dilute the oil
and hold it up to the moon, saying:

you will need:
sandalwood oil dissolved
in carrier oil, two drops
per teaspoon

a large, soft gold cloth

a gold candle

a sachet of St. John's
Wort tea

some honey

"Lady moon, heal my heart.
Yemaya of the tides, take me to fresh waters."

Sit on the gold cloth with the candles burning around
you, and your mug of hot tea and honey beside you. If the
moon is shining, so much the better. Sip your tea. Rub the
oil lovingly into your skin, especially near your heart. Feel
warmth growing behind your navel, spreading into your
chest and over your heart, soothing, healing. Think of all the
positive things you have in life. Imagine new and better
times sailing your way. Repeat as often as you like, until your
heart is healed and sunshine comes back into your life.

credits

David Montgomery 2, 3, 5 ar, 5 b, 6–7, 12, 13 background, 14–15, 18, 26, 27 ar, 32, 33, 38, 39, 42–43, 49, 64, endpapers
David Brittain 5 al, 13, 20, 30 l, 30 ar, 58–59

Sandra Lane 4 c, 16, 52, 55
Dan Duchars 30 br, 50–51, 56
Chris Tubbs 11, 24–25, 63
Chris Everard 34, 35, 37
Polly Wreford 19, 47, 54
Caroline Arber 1, 27 al
Jan Baldwin 22–23, 41

Catherine Gratwicke 4 b, 29
Tom Leighton 4 a, 45
William Lingwood 44, 60–61
James Merrell 27 bl & r
Alan Williams 48
Francesca Yorke 8–9